AF231213

*Unlock the flow and effectiveness of
your Church Bereavement Ministry
with included customized
"First Call" forms*

Create Your Own Bereavement Ministry

Includes Customizable Guides and Forms

Thelma Manning Hall, Ph. D.

Create Your Own Bereavement Ministry

© 2021 by Thelma Manning Hall, Ph.D.

All rights reserved.

No portion of this book may be reproduced, stored in a retrieval system, or transmitted in any form or by means of electronic, mechanical, photocopy, recording, scanning, or another excerpt for brief quotations in critical reviews or articles, without the prior written permission of the publisher.

ISBN: 978-1-955622-95-0

Published by

Fideli Publishing, Inc.
119 W. Morgan St.
Martinsville, IN 46151

www.FideliPublishing.com

PRINTED IN THE UNITED STATES OF AMERICA

Dedication

This book is dedicated to my family who have transitioned. My family have contributed to my success in life from my cradle until their demise.

My grandfather, Nathaniel Wofford, Sr., and my grandmother, Ella Shaffer Wofford and their children have always encouraged me. There was never a time when they did not ask my mother, "What is she studying now?"

My grandparent's children are Mattie Wofford Gray; Sarah Wofford Stone, L. E. Wofford, Nathaniel Wofford, Jr., Johnnie Wofford, J.V. Wofford, Willie Wofford and Gavie Wofford and my siblings: Felix Gray, Jr and Melvin Gray are held dearly in my heart.

I dedicate this book to precious memories of my beloved mother, Mrs. Mattie Mae Wofford Gray, who supported me in all my endeavors. This is one of her many expressions of appreciation and love for her daughter expressed in an Ambassador Card prior to her transitioning.

*"**Dear Daughter,***

It's easy to take things for granted in a family,

to assume that you just know the things that somehow never get said...

... But maybe you don't know how special you are,

how easy it is to be proud of you.

Maybe you don't realize how much it's always meant

to have you for a daughter,

to see you grow up so beautifully

without ever growing away from those who love you.

Well, in case you don't know,

this is coming just to tell you what a wonderful daughter you are —

and how much you are loved.

From Your Mother and Family — Sisters and Brothers, With love

Acknowledgments

The birth of this book is from many years of experience acquired through church leadership at the Indiana Avenue Pentecostal Church of God, Chicago, Illinois, as a Sunday School Teacher, and Primary Superintendent, Radio Announcer, Usher, Secretary of the Choir, and The Church Secretary.

I thank the patriots of my past and acknowledge, from my humble beginning, the late Bishop Charles Edward Davis, pastor of the Indiana Avenue Pentecostal Church of God, Inc., Chicago, Illinois, whose expectation of me was nothing less than perfection.

Much appreciation for the late Elder Odee Akines, pastor of the Indiana Avenue Pentecostal Church of God, Inc., Chicago, Illinois, who had confidence in my ability and who gave me the freedom to compose his correspondence from the dignitaries of the City of Chicago and the State of Illinois. In addition to secretarial duties, a file was prepared for the seniors, in advance of their transition, and their plans for the funeral programs were kept on file.

Thankful for the insight and the vision of Bishop Clinton House, pastor of Mountaintop Faith Ministries, Las Vegas, Nevada, who appointed me as the church licensed funeral director, and the Director of Bereavement Ministry.

Acknowledging the Bereavement Ministry subleaders, Eleanor Smith, Nora Spann, Richard Johnson, Glen Franklin, Elizabeth Valentino and Eileen Baggett Jackson, in their respective positions, without their leadership, the Funeral Process would not run smoothly at Mountaintop Faith Ministries. My hearty thanks for their faithfulness to God and their attentiveness to details in caring for the bereaved families.

Special acknowledgement to the Bereavement Ministry Team of 36 volunteers for their faithfulness as servants of God. These servants are all Comfort Specialist and are used of God to comfort families who have lost their loved ones.

My love and appreciation to my husband, Charles Hall, Jr., for his patience with me while writing this book for all the churches and pastors around the world.

My hearty thanks to my publisher, Robin Surface, for her diligence in making this book a reality.

Table of Contents

PART II: FORMS FOR CREATING YOUR OWN BEREAVEMENT MINISTRY

Preface

Individualize Your Ministry

Part I of this book is to be used as a guide. A copy should be utilized in all churches and tailored to your church or wherever funeral services are held. However, the bereavement ministry service has proven to be useful to pastors and leaders in any church. The First Call Sheets are highly recommended for churches of all denominations. Part II provides forms to be completed and tailored to your church and its programs.

This book will benefit pastors, ministers, deacons, greeters, ushers, health professionals, production staff and special needs ministry who work with family members during the funeral service.

By including all of the supporting church ministries in the funeral process, the flow of the service will be well organized. There should be a copy of *Create Your Own Bereavement Ministry* in every church.

In the Forms Section, the First Call Sheets will start the information process from the bereaved family member to the Church. The First Call Sheets are listed separately and can be used only if needed. There are seven sections:

Part I. Information received from the first call form

Part II. Information on the Deceased

Part III. Information received if church member

Part IV. Information needed for planning church funeral

Part V. Information needed for Funeral Service

Part VI. Information for Catering Meal

Part VII. Information for Repast

Part I, II, IV, V are definitely needed. Part III, VI, VII may or may not be applicable to every family.

The Check List. This is a list of items and volunteers needed for the funeral service.

Part I — The set-up persons will be responsible for podium, table, easels, placing memorial registration book.

Part II — The checklist includes ministries needed to be sure the funeral service is well-staffed with ministers, deacons, greeters, ushers, health professionals, production staff and the ministry for special needs (ADA).

There are other forms for informational purposes in the Forms Section of this book starting on page 35.

Our Mission:

To Comfort the Family

To provide bereaved families with comfort, love, encouragement and guidance. As vessels, we are praying for the family that God will comfort them through the word of God.

To be Compassionate

To minister to the bereaved family with compassion, discernment and understanding, during their difficult time of loss.

To Empower the Family

To empower the bereaved family with the Word of God to help them during their hours of grief.

To Challenge the Family

To challenge the bereaved family to believe the word of God; to believe that peace can only come from God. God promised that He will never leave nor forsake us. God will give the oil of joy for mourning and the garment of praise for the spirit of heaviness. God promises love, peace and a sound mind.

SECTION I

Understanding the Components of a Bereavement Ministry

²⁸Hast thou not known?
hast thou not heard, that the everlasting God, the Lord,
the Creator of the ends of the earth, fainteth not, neither is weary?
there is no searching of His understanding.

²⁹He giveth power to the faint;
and to them that have no might He increaseth strength.
³⁰Even the youths shall faint and be weary,
and the young men shall utterly fall:

³¹But they that wait upon the Lord shall renew their strength;
they shall mount up with wings as eagles;
they shall run, and not be weary;
and they shall walk, and not faint.

— Isaiah 40:28–31 (KJV)

The Grief Process

Grief is a natural process. We experience grief when we lose someone. Many of us have experienced the loss of a loved one. Do we understand the grieving process?

The definition of grief is: The intense emotional suffering caused by a loss. Grief affects how we feel and our state of mind. To mourn is to express those feelings.

STAGES OF GRIEF:

There is a process of grieving associated with loss. These stages are important for all to know in order to help people go through what is referred to as a "normal grieving process." Some people may not experience all of the stages of grief. Some people may not experience the stages of grief as another person.

In his book, *Good Grief,* the late pastor and teacher Granger E. Westberg identifies ten (10) stages of grief:

1. Shock is a temporary escape.

2. Emotional reaction is to release.

3. Depression is a form of loneliness.

4. Physical distress is despair.

5. Panic is fear.

6. Guilt is feelings of regret.

7. Anger is to place blame.

8. Resistance is refusal to return to normal.

9. Hope is gradually returning back to life again.

10. Acceptance is to affirm reality.

The Church Bereavement Ministry

The death of a loved one is an intense and painful experience for most people. The Church is the first source for detailed guidance on planning a funeral service. The minister is the vessel for Jesus Christ and is the vessel God has empowered to provide the bereaved family with words of comfort, love, encouragement and guidance to help them get through the process of losing a loved one.

The Church Bereavement Ministry is an excellent resource for pastors to embrace when families have needs. There are many faucets of the funeral process. The Bereavement Ministry can help pastors and the family ease worry, stress, and anxiety.

Having the right support during this time can make a difference. Prayer and fasting are essential tools when consoling the family.

Implementing the Bereavement Ministry will help ensure that attention is administered to the family in an orderly manner based on their needs. Each family has unique specifications. No funeral service is the same.

The funeral director, chosen by the family, will contact the pastor of the church and obtain information as to designated area where the family will be seated. On the day of the funeral service, those instructions will be carried out. The funeral director will set up procedures in accordance with the Pastor's instructions.

To start the process of planning a church funeral service, let us create a flow chart. The flow chart is key to communication. Everyone has a specific assignment. When the information is properly disseminated, the funeral service will be carried out without confusion.

The Bereavement Ministry Flowchart

(To Be Used as a Guide)

CONTACT	➜	ACTION
Bereaved Family Member	➜	contacts the Church.
Church Bereavement Care Person	➜	completes the **First Call Form** (see froms section, page 37).
Church Bereavement Care Person	➜	coordinates dates with the **Church Administrator.**
Church Bereavement Care Person	➜	coordinates the **Church's** available dates with the funeral home.
Church Bereavement Care Person	➜	validates availability of all ministries for the scheduled bereavement service.
Church Bereavement Care Person	➜	follows up on information obtained from the bereaved's family member(s).
Church Bereavement Care Person	➜	disseminates information to responsible ministries for the funeral service.
Church Bereavement Care Person	➜	uses **Check List** (see page 45) information to activate supporting ministries as needed.
Church Bereavement Care Person	➜	notifies the **Bereavement Ministry Coordinator** who sends out the notices to the **Bereavement Ministry Members.**

Bereavement Ministry Procedures

(To Be Used as a Guide)

FAMILY:

The Church Bereavement Care Person or designated lead person will contact the bereaved family. The family may request help with preparation for putting the program together or writing the obituary, or the complete planning of a funeral service to include repast information.

The First Call Form, reflects the family's needs, and will be forwarded to the Church Bereavement Care Person reflects the family's needs, and will be forwarded for necessary actions. (See page 35 in the Forms Section)

If the Church Bereavement Care Person or designated lead person recognizes one or more of the stages of grief, such as anger, guilt or depression, the Bereavement Ministry Coordinator will refer this information to the Senior Care Person or the Pastor.

BEREAVEMENT CARE PERSON:

The **Church Bereavement Care Person** will confirm the service, date and times with the **Church Administrator.**

The **Church Care Person** will determine the need for number of persons within a ministry required to participate in all funeral services, i.e. one minister, two deacons, two ushers, two greeters, to work with the Bereavement Ministry members.

SUPPORTING MINISTRIES:

The **Administrator** will designate the **Church Bereavement Care Person** who contacts the **Supporting Ministries** by email.

The **Church Bereavement Ministry Coordinators** or designated lead person will use the Checklist form (See Forms Section page 45) to activate supporting ministries and report the assignment of their members as to whom will be working the funeral service.

The Supporting Ministries Checklist may consist of the following: *Ministers, Operations, Musicians, Sanctuary Attendants, Deacon Board, Senior Eagles in Action Ministry, Health Professional Ministry, Greeters Ministry, Special Needs Ministry and other assigned ministries as needed.*

BEREAVEMENT MINISTRY ASSIGNMENT:

The **Church Bereavement Care Person** will contact the members of the **Bereavement Ministry.** Members of the Bereavement Ministry are assigned based upon availability and will make other assignments to fulfill the bereaved family's needs.

Bereavement Ministry Funeral Assignments

(To Be Used as a Guide)

The Order of Funeral Service Duties

BEFORE THE SERVICE:

- Designated person(s) will set up the sanctuary before the service for a traditional or a memorial service and afterwards the funeral service, return church to its original setting.

- Designated person(s) will be responsible for setting out the waste paper baskets, water, and boxes of Kleenex.

- Designated person will be responsible for distribution of badges at the beginning of the funeral service for sign in and sign out of the Bereavement Ministry badges.

- Designated person(s) will meet with the family in a holding area: provide Kleenex, water for the bereaved family.

- Designated person will coordinate with funeral directors concerning the Memorial Registry Book, and Funeral Programs.

- Designated person(s) will coordinate with Church Bereavement Care Person as to who is the assigned minister to have prayer with the family; Lead the processional of the family to enter the sanctuary.

- Designated person(s) will coordinate the seating by row in the sanctuary.
- Designated person(s) will be responsible for getting the Memorial Book and Cards to proper family member.

PRAYER BEFORE THE SERVICE BEGINS BY THE ENTIRE GROUP

The entire Bereavement Ministry members will pray. After the prayer, the Bereavement Ministry Coordinator or designated lead person will assign duties to be performed before the funeral service.

THE BEGINNING OF SERVICE

A designated person(s) will make assignments at the beginning of the funeral service. Bereavement Members can perform in positions as: Ushers, Greeters, and stand at the Memorial Register Book.

DURING THE SERVICE

The remaining members are assigned to rotate and will attend to the needs of the bereaved family. Rotation to stand at every other row in intervals of 10 minutes.

THE END OF THE SERVICE

A designated person(s) will assign the brothers and sisters to line up to carry out the flowers. A designated person(s) will assign the Bereavement brothers to fill in as pallbearers when needed.

DATABASE MINISTRY

The Church Bereavement Care Person will submit a copy of the Funeral Service Program to the Database Ministry to update the church records.

Traditional Funeral Service Standard Operating Procedures (SOP)

(To Be Used as a Guide)

Church Bereavement Ministry or Facilitator

A. PRIOR TO DAY OF FUNERAL:

1. **Call Family Member.** Ask family to provide information needed at Church, and have prayer with specified family member.

2. **Call Funeral Home** to obtain time remains will arrive at Church.

3. **Notify Safety Ministry** (Safety Team) to direct the hearse to proper entry door.

B. CALL FAMILY TO COORDINATE WHAT CHURCH NEEDS:

1. Music and/or Production Ministries Video, DVD, CD.

2. **Information Needed from Family:**

   • Obtain Program

   • Picture

   • Memorial Registry Book

- Number of expected family members attending service. Reserve seating by row and total number expected in attendance to determine the size of the facility needed to accommodate the service.

C. SEND OUT E-MAIL NOTICES TO ALL BEREAVEMENT MINISTRY MEMBERS:

The response will determine how many members will be present to console the family.

D. THE DAY OF FUNERAL SERVICE. FACILITATOR WILL:

1. **Arrive at the Church one-hour prior to scheduled funeral time.**
2. **Coordinate with facility and operation person** to obtain the podium and easel.
3. **Coordinate with facility staff** to obtain Bereavement Ministry items, water, baskets, badges, Kleenex, etc.
4. **Coordinate with the Deacons** for opening the doors for the arrival of hearse. Unlock doors to obtain supplies.

E. FACILITATOR PERFORMS OTHER DUTIES AS NEEDED:

1. **Sign for and Receive Floral Arrangements** sent to the Church.
2. **Arrange flowers** with the permission of the funeral director if needed.
   a. Flowers from the family are placed at the head of the casket.
   b. Flowers from friends are placed at the foot of the casket.

Parts of a Traditional Funeral Service

PART I

CHURCH BEREAVEMENT MINISTRY COORDINATOR
(THE PASTOR'S POINT PERSON) COORDINATES WITH ALL STAFF PERSONNEL

A. All Ministry Staff are requested to arrive 30 minutes prior to funeral service time.

B. Wear black suits and white blouses for women; black suits and white shirts for men.

C. Have prayer with all staff present and assign positions.

PART II

DUTIES FOR EACH MINISTRY AT A TRADITIONAL FUNERAL SERVICE

1. CORPORATE STAFF DUTIES

A. Receives the call, Senior Care Person will follow up with the family.

B. Send information to Facilitator and Bereavement Coordinator.

C. Prepare the Condolence for the family's funeral service.

D. Proofread obituary received from the family.

E. Prepare funeral program if needed.

F. Obtain information for meal (Number of people, time and place of delivery).

G. Use **Ministry Check List** (see page 10) to determine ministries needed for each funeral service.

F. Monitor and grant special request from the family.

2. CHURCH FACILITIES OR OPERATIONS DUTIES

A. Will vacuum, dust, check bathrooms for paper towels, etc.

B. Will set up the sanctuary for the funeral service.

C. Will check proper temperature of room.

D. Will put Kleenex, baskets, water on the table for easy access.

E. Will place easels, podiums in proper locations.

D. Will perform other duties as assigned.

3. SAFETY MINISTRY (SAFETY TEAM):

A. Will direct the driver of the hearse to the proper door per the Church Coordinator's instructions.

B. Along with Deacons will interact or over-lap in absence of Safety Ministry.

C. Will man the parking lot for safety of operations of funeral cars, line up of cars.

D. Will place traffic cones for directing the traffic flow and/or parking.

E. Will move around the campus property to detect suspicious persons or situations.

F. Will ensure that all thermostats are set at 75 degrees.

G. Will ensure that all TV Monitors and all Electronics are turned off, i.e., organ and keyboard, etc.

H. Will reset the alarm at end of funeral service, if applicable.

4. DEACON BOARD (DEACONS OR DEACONS-IN-TRAINING)

A. The Church Deacons are assigned by the Head Deacon to attend the funeral service.

B. Deacons are assigned to help guest up and down stairs to the podium when program calls for making remarks.

C. The duties will vary as follows:

1. Open the proper door of the Church; Check or adjust room temperature of sanctuary.
2. In the absence of the Deacons, the Safety Ministry will direct the funeral car to the proper door based on location of the service; will be held; Add folding chairs if there is an overflow in attendance.
3. Unlock doors so the various ministries can get their supplies for a funeral service
4. Obtain podium, easels, etc., and place in proper location(s).
5. Be alert while monitoring the Hall Ways during the funeral service.
6. Check the parking area, along with the Safety Ministry, when cars are arriving or departing.

5. BEREAVEMENT MINISTRY:

A. Prior to the start of funeral service, the Bereavement Ministry will prepare for the set-up placing Kleenex, water and baskets in the first three (3) rows based on the number of family members.

B. One Bereavement Ministry member will be assigned to stand at the Memorial Registry Book in the lobby.

C. The Bereavement Ministry will administer comfort to the family in a spirit of excellence; provide Kleenex or removal of soiled Kleenex from the hands of family members; and family member place soiled Kleenex in a small basket for disposal, provide water; escort a family member to the area of restrooms and escort them back to their seat. Provide information to family as needed basis, i.e., this facility is non-smoking.

D. Four to six Bereavement Ministry members are expected to be present at all funeral services. If the service is small four to six members are present. If the funeral service is large ten to twelve bereavement members are expected to be present. New members who are, in training, are requested to attend funeral services for observation.

E. One person is the person in charge to make assignments; one person is responsible for members who will sign-in, and assign badges at beginning of funeral service and sign-out and collect badges at the end of a funeral service.

6. GREETERS:

A. The Bereavement Ministry Coordinator will assign the Greeters to a position in the absence of their Ministry Director.

B. Greeters Ministry will be assigned positions and will administer information, with a big smile, to the guest upon arrival;

C. Point the guest to the location of the funeral service;

D. In some instances, ask if a member of the family to further direct family to the proper holding location.

E. If a small funeral service, a minimum of two greeters are expected to be present. If the funeral service is large, a minimum of four greeters are expected to be present.

F. A good time for **Greeters** to leave their position is before the obituary is read.

7. SANCTUARY ATTENDANTS (USHERS)

A. **Sanctuary Attendants** will be assigned to their position; one at the Door, and one in the Center Isle.

B. If the attendance for the funeral service is large, at least four ushers will be required.

C. The Sanctuary Attendants will locate seats for the guest and order the seating of the audience i.e., special assigned or special seating arrangement for ministries — Deacons, Deacons' Wives, Choir, etc.

D. This information is given to the Sanctuary Attendants (Ushers) upon their arrival.

E. **Process for Departing View:** Sanctuary Attendants (Ushers) will direct the Section to the right, or <u>the foot of the casket</u> and start with the last row; request <u>row</u> to stand, proceed out to the <u>right.</u>

OPTION: The people may leave the sanctuary or return to their seats.

F. The Center Section will stand, proceed out to the Right and go around to the <u>foot of the casket</u>.

OPTION: The people may leave or return to their seats.

<u>NOTE</u>: *If the First Section is going down the Center Isle, the second section cannot go up the same isle. They must follow the flow of the people before them.*

8. MINISTERS

The Ministers who are assigned to attend the funeral service, will arrive 30 minutes prior to the scheduled time of the funeral service; will have prayers with all the Staff. The Ministers are assigned to a designated area.

Program Seating Arrangements:

1. You are assigned seating convenient to easily get to the microphone and it helps the program to flow smoothly.

2. **Program Participants:** Persons identified as on program will be placed in a designated area.

3. **Pallbearers:** Pallbearers are seated on the first row to the right of casket.

   <u>NOTE</u>: Seating is subject to change.

9. MUSIC MINISTRY:

A. Based upon the family's request, a song will be provided.

B. If family has no specific song, the Music Director will select an appropriate song.

C. Music Director will select a psalmist to render selection(s).

D. Make sure that all songs are appropriate for funeral services.

10. PRODUCTION MINISTRY:

A. Family requested to submit 2 to 5-minute video, DVD or CD.

B. Family may request a videotaped copy of funeral service based on availability of staff.

C. Production Ministry will play soft music prior to the start time of the funeral service.

D. Production Ministry will test the video, DVD, CD submitted by the family, two days prior to the Funeral Service. Testing is to ensure it can be played on Church equipment.

E. Production Ministry can use internet technology to locate requested music if CD does not work on Church equipment.

F. Production Ministry will check the sound system.

G. Production Ministry will place microphones in proper positions prior to start of funeral service.

11. (FIRST AID MINISTRY (HEALTH PROFESSIONAL)

A. Will come prepared to serve the bereaved family;

B. Will be assigned a designated position near the family.

C. Will remain alert by keeping the family in view.

D. Will look for unusual body signs of stress.

12. SPECIAL NEEDS MINISTRY:

1. Will be assigned to the first row to the right section nearest to the door of the sanctuary.
2. The sanctuary will be set up by the Operations Ministry to accommodate the Special Needs Ministry as needed.
3. Will coordinate the pick-up schedule with the RTC Bus Schedule for the Special Needs members.
4. Will assist the Special Needs members with their individual needs, i.e., medication, water, restroom breaks, diabetics with snacks, etc.
5. At no time will the Special Needs Ministry members assume responsibility for administering medication. If this rule is not observed, it is a possible liability for the Church.

PART III

TRADITIONAL CHURCH FUNERAL SERVICE

Sometimes, there is a scheduled visitation at the Church before the funeral service starts.

VISITATION BEFORE SERVICE

If viewing before service starts, the casket is open until time for the service to begin. The purpose for closing the casket during the funeral service program is to show respect to the family and maintain order during the service.

PROCESSIONAL LINE-UP FOR THE SERVICE

Upon the start of the service, the line-up for the processional:

Protocol for entering the sanctuary:

Funeral Director will request the family to line up in twos.

The person paying the bill is seated on the first pew, first seat and the nearest of kin to follow.

Seating Position: The nearest of kin to follow until all the family is seated.

OPTIONAL: Based on instructions received from the Pastor, some churches allow funeral directors to lead family into the sanctuary and seat the family without a minister.

PROCESSIONAL ENTERING THE SANCTUARY

1. Pastor and Ministers lead the family

2. Minister reads scripture(s): Division of Psalms 23, 25, 27

3. All in line-up will walk slowly until pastor reaches the designated seats at the head of the casket which are reserved for the family.

4. Funeral director will seat the family on the first pew.

5. All other family members will be seated on the second pew and thereafter until all the family is seated.

6. Family is requested to fill each seat on every row; provide this information to the family while in the family-holding area.

CHURCH PARTING VIEW PROTOCOL

At the conclusion of the Eulogy, the funeral Director will come forward to prepare remains for the departing view.

ORDER OF PARTING VIEWING:

At the direction of the funeral director:

1. The ministers start the viewing process and should walk beginning from foot of casket to head of the casket, and may stand at head of casket or as directed by the pastor.

2. The right side of the Congregation. The ushers will continue the viewing process. And will direct the congregation by pew, beginning at the last row; direct congregation to walk around to the foot of the casket, proceed to the head of the casket, and return to their seats.

3. The left side of congregation, the ushers will direct congregants by pew from the last row to walk around to the foot of the casket and proceed to the head of the casket and return to their seats.

4. The Funeral Director will personally attend to the immediate family for the final departing view.

5. The Bereavement Ministry men will line up to remove the heavy funeral florals. Men will give vase or smaller plants to women. Men will carry the heavy floral pots or floral on easels.

6. At the conclusion of immediate family viewing, the funeral director will call for the six pallbearers.

7. Committal: Grave Side ceremony can be performed prior to leaving sanctuary for cemetery.

8. The minister will lead the casket out of the church, one funeral director will follow in front of casket and the pallbearers will take their positions, three on each side of the casket. The second funeral director will escort the family and follow behind the casket out of sanctuary.

9. Family members and guests who will drive to grave site, should proceed to their cars and turn their lights on if participating in funeral processional to grave site and instruct all drivers to obey the law and do not run red lights.

   NOTE: If the information is omitted from the program, the funeral director will obtain instructions from the family concerning the departing view.

Qualifications and Duties of Members

(To Be Used as a Guide)

AS BEREAVEMENT MINISTRY MEMBERS:

- Do you pray and fast corporately and individually, so that you are in tune with God and in compliance with Church rules and procedures?

- Are you faithful in attendance at all Bereavement Ministry meetings?

- Do you suggest positive solutions that will help the ministry to be effective and work with a spirit of excellence?

- Do you study and know the stages of grief and how to console and how to support the bereaved?

- Do you serve with grace, show compassion, give words of comfort to those who are bereaved?

- Do you give words of encouragement practicing the "What to Say and What Not to Say"?

- Do you pray continually for all bereaved family members?

Suggested reading: John 3:3, Acts 2:4, Acts 2:38.

DRESS CODE:

Remember, this is a Bereavement Ministry. Therefore, when attending a funeral service, the following applies:

Women:

- Black suit and white blouse in Spring, Summer, Fall and Winter.
- Comfortable shoes; no sports shoes; no flip flops.
- No pants

Men:

- Black suit and white dress shirt, black tie.
- Comfortable shoes; no sports shoes; no flip flops.

  <u>**NOTE**</u>: All Members will be distributed badges before the service, which will be collected immediately following the service.

I Thessalonians 4:13-18 NIV

[13]Brothers and sisters, we do not want you to be uninformed about those who sleep in death, so that you do not grieve like the rest of mankind, who have no hope.

[14]For we believe that Jesus died and rose again, and so we believe that God will bring with Jesus those who have fallen asleep in him.

[15]According to the Lord's word, we tell you that we who are still alive, who are left until the coming of the Lord, will certainly not precede those who have fallen asleep.

[16]For the Lord himself will come down from heaven, with a loud command, with the voice of the archangel and with the trumpet call of God, and the dead in Christ will rise first.

[17]After that, we who are still alive and are left will be caught up together with them in the clouds to meet the Lord in the air. And so we will be with the Lord forever.

[18]Therefore encourage one another with these words.

Traditional and Memorial Funeral Services provide the bereaved family a place to express their feelings of grief and loss. It is a time to remember a life and recognize that your loved one has lived and influenced many people during their life.

The service is an extremely emotional time for the family. As Ministry members, our service to the bereaved family is to offer support, compassion, comfort and encouragement.

Memorial and Traditional Services

(To Be Used as a Guide)

SERVICES HELD AT THE CHURCH:

- Bereavement Ministry workers are positioned to stand at the left and right of specific rows to attend to the needs of the family.

- Bereavement Ministry workers are to provide comfort (i.e., facial tissue or water) and assist family members to the hallway or outside for fresh air, if desired.

- In some instances, the Bereavement Ministry worker may be asked to escort the bereaved family member to various locations outside the sanctuary.

- Bereavement Ministry workers are positioned to assist family members during the viewing, which can be a particularly intense experience for family members.

- All available Bereavement Ministry workers are required to attend the funeral services for on-going training. Each funeral service is different and no two funeral services are alike.

SERVICES HELD OFF-SITE:

- The Bereavement Ministry will not wear their uniform to off-site funeral services unless directed by Pastor as follows:

- **Another Church:** Services held at another church as the primary responsibility of the designated staff member. The Bereavement Ministry can attend off-site services to support the family, but not to service the family.

- **Mortuary**: Services held at a mortuary are the primary responsibility of the mortuary staff. The Bereavement Ministry can attend the service, to support the family member, but not to serve the family. Special arrangements can be requested by the family and granted.

SERVICES HELD OUT OF STATE:

- The Church Bereavement Care Person may be asked to contact the bereaved family.

- The Church Bereavement Care Person may be asked to pray and offer condolence on behalf of the Church.

- The Church Bereavement Care Person will send a condolence to the family from the Church.

EACH SERVICE IS DIFFERENT:

- Prior to serving, the Bereavement Ministry Coordinator will pray.

- Each service is different and *all procedures listed may or may not be needed.*

- Follow the directions and the instructions of the Bereavement Ministry Coordinator or the designated lead person.

REPAST PROCEDURES

The bereaved family, friends and associates come together at a place where food and drinks are shared along with memories to celebrate the life of their loved one. Repast can be held at the church or at a banquet hall.

CHURCH CULINARY/CATERING:

Meals Delivered to Bereaved Family Home:

- One meal can be delivered to the bereaved family, generally the evening prior to the service.
- The Administrator or the Church Bereavement Care Person will verify with the family, if there are any food allergies and confirm the time and place for the meal delivery.
- The Senior Care Person will notify the designated caterer of the time and place the meal is to be delivered.
- The caterer will deliver the meal to the designated location.

Consoling the Bereaved
What We Should Say and Should Not Say
(To Be Used as a Guide)

There are common clichés spoken to bereaved individuals that actually do more harm than good. Here are some suggestions to assist you when talking or writing to someone you are consoling during their time of loss:

DON'T SAY:	SAY INSTEAD:
I know just how you feel…	*I know you are hurting…*
At least he's out of pain…	*Say nothing about the pain, just listen…*
You're still young; you can have another baby.	*Never suggest that a person could replace a baby (or even a pet).*
It was God's will…	*God will comfort you… (Matt 5:4)*
Buck up; you have to be strong now…	*Trust in God for your strength. He'll supply everything you need to get you through each day, one day at a time. Just ask God and be specific:* *"Lord, help me make the funeral arrangements," and "Lord, give me the strength to notify the family," etc.*

DON'T SAY:	SAY INSTEAD:
He/she wouldn't want you to cry…	*It is okay to cry. (Smile when saying this and offer a hug if appropriate.)*
Let me tell you what I went through…	*Leave your personal experience out of the conversation; if the bereaved asks about it, limit the discussion and put the focus back on him or her.*
If there's anything I can do, just let me know…	*Don't ask; just do it. A grieving person will rarely ask for help, but he/she will gladly accept it.*
It's been six months since he died, it's time to get on with your life…	*The amount of time a person takes to go through the grieving process is personal. There is no right or wrong amount of time to grieve.*
You should get rid of all her things. Having them around just keeps you sad.	*Again, the amount of time a person takes to grieve is different and is an individual's choice. Sometimes photos and personal belongings are pleasant reminders. Ask the Holy Spirit to guide you. If the person appears depressed or immobilized, you want to lovingly suggest counseling or other help.*
She went to sleep and the angels took her away.	*Never say this. Children may begin to fear sleeping and avoid facing the truth.*

AUTHOR UNKNOWN

SECTION II

Forms for Customizing and Creating Your Own Bereavement Ministry

Bereavement Ministry Flowchart

CONTACT	➜	ACTION
Bereaved Family Member _________________________ NAME _________________________ PHONE NUMBER _________________________ EMAIL	➜	contacts the Church: _________________________ CHURCH NAME _________________________ PHONE NUMBER _________________________ EMAIL
Church Bereavement Care Person _________________________ NAME _________________________ PHONE NUMBER _________________________ EMAIL	➜ ➜ ➜ ➜	completes the **First Call Form** (see froms section, page 37). coordinates dates with the **Church Administrator.** coordinates the **Church's** available dates with the funeral home. validates availability of all ministries for the scheduled bereavement service.
Church Bereavement Care Person _________________________ NAME _________________________ PHONE NUMBER _________________________ EMAIL	➜ ➜	follows up on information obtained from the bereaved family member. disseminates information to responsible ministries for the funeral service.
Church Bereavement Care Person _________________________ NAME _________________________ PHONE NUMBER _________________________ EMAIL	➜ ➜	uses **Check List** (see page 45) information to activate supporting ministries as needed. notifies the **Bereavement Ministry Coordinator** who sends out the notices to the **Bereavement Ministry Members.**

Bereavement First Call Sheet
(May be customized as needed)

Date_____________________ Time _________________ am/pm   Case # _________________

NOTE: *Upon receipt of first call, office staff will notify the Church Bereavement Care Person for the Bereavement Ministry.*

PART I - INFORMATION FROM FIRST CALL:

Name of Caller ____

Phone # _________________________________ Cell # _______________________________

Primary Responsible Party ____

Relationship ____

Address ____

City _________________________________State _____________ Zip Code ____________

Other Contact ____

Phone # ____

Address ____

City _________________________________State _____________ Zip Code ____________

How are you related to the deceased? ____

Are you the person responsible for decisions on behalf of the family? /___/ Yes /___/ No

NOTE: *If no, request responsible person to call the Church with information concerning the deceased.*

Are you the person responsible for payment of the funeral bill? /___/ Yes /___/ No

PART II - INFORMATION ON THE DECEASED

Name of Deceased ____

Address of Deceased ____

City ___________________________________State _______________ Zip Code ___________

Date of Death _______________________________Place of Death _______________________________

/_____/ Ship In ____

(When your loved one is transported from another State to your State.)

/_____/ Ship Out ____

(When you tell the Mortuary you want your loved one transported to another mortuary in another State.)

Have you contacted a Funeral Home? /____/ Yes /____/ No

(If yes, provide information the following information:

Name of Funeral Home____

Address of Funeral Home ____

City ___________________________________State _______________ Zip Code ___________

PART III - INFORMATION ON CHURCH MEMBERS

Was the deceased a member of this Church? /___/ **Yes** /___/ **No**

Are there family members of this Church? /___/ **Yes** /___/ **No**

If yes, provide names of family member(s):

Name ____

Address ____

____

City ____

State ____________ **Zip Code** ____________________

Phone ____

Cell ____

____

Name ____

Address ____

____

City ____

State ____________ **Zip Code** ____________________

Phone ____

Cell ____

____

Name ____

Address ____

____

City ____

State ____________ **Zip Code** ____________________

Phone ____

Cell ____

____

Name ____

Address ____

____

City ____

State ____________ **Zip Code** ____________________

Phone ____

Cell ____

____

Name ____

Address ____

____

City ____

State ____________ **Zip Code** ____________________

Phone ____

Cell ____

____

Name ____

Address ____

____

City ____

State ____________ **Zip Code** ____________________

Phone ____

Cell ____

____

Name _______________________________________

Address ____________________________________

____

City ____

State _______________ **Zip Code** __________________

Phone _______________________________________

Cell ____

____

Name _______________________________________

Address ____________________________________

____

City ____

State _______________ **Zip Code** __________________

Phone _______________________________________

Cell ____

____

Name _______________________________________

Address ____________________________________

____

City ____

State _______________ **Zip Code** __________________

Phone _______________________________________

Cell ____

____

NOTE: *Use separate sheet for additional names, addresses, City/State/zip code.*

PART IV — INFORMATION FOR PLANNING FUNERAL SERVICE

NOTE: *Coordinate the funeral dates with funeral home and the desired church.*

PREFERRED LOCATION OF SERVICE

Address ____

____

City ____

State ______________ Zip Code __________________

Phone ____

FAMILY'S PREFERRED SERVICE DATE

DATE ____

TIME ____

NOTE: Validate and Coordinate Dates

FAMILY'S PREFERRED VISITATION DATE/TIME

DATE ____

TIME ____

NOTE: Validate and Coordinate Dates

ALTERNATE LOCATION

Address ____

____

City ____

State ______________ Zip Code __________________

Phone ____

CHURCH CALENDAR AVAILABILITY

DATE ____

TIME ____

FUNERAL HOME AVAILABILITY

DATE ____

TIME ____

CHURCH CALENDAR AVAILABILITY

DATE ____

TIME ____

FUNERAL HOME AVAILABILITY

DATE ____

TIME ____

Officiating Minister's Name ____

Phone ___________________________ Cell ___________________________

Visiting Minister's Name ____

City ___________________________________ State ______ Zip Code ________

Phone ___________________________ Cell ___________________________

NOTE: *Call or meet with the family at their home to obtain additional information, to show concern, to console and to pray with the family.*

PART V – INFORMATION FOR FUNERAL SERVICE

What type of service are you considering? (Please indicate)

Traditional Funeral Service /______/

Direct Burial /______/

Memorial Funeral Service /______/

Graveside /______/

Direct Cremation /______/

Anatomical Donation /______/

VETERANS:

Was the deceased a Veteran? /___/ Yes /___/ No

Was Your Loved One a Retired Veteran? /___/ Yes /___/ No

Does your Retired Veteran require a 21-gun salute? /___/ Yes /___/ No

Name of Cemetery ____

Address ____

City ____ State ____________ Zip Code ________________

Phone ____

Has the family designated someone to write the obituary? /___/ Yes /___/ No

Specify the number of easels ______________________

FAMILY SEATING ARRANGEMENTS:

Seating of Family ______________ Expected Family Out of Town __________

Numbers of rows to reserve __________

PART VI – CATERING INFORMATION

Provide the following information for delivery of Catered Meal:

LOCATION, DATE AND TIME FOR THE MEAL:

Address ____

____

City ____State _______Zip Code ___________

Contact name____

Phone ____

Date _______________________________ Time _________________________________

<u>NOTE:</u> Be sure to specify the desired menu type and make known any allergies.

PART VII – REPAST INFORMATION

Has the family secured a facility for the repast? /___/ Yes /___/ No

Will the repast information be included on the program? /___/ Yes /___/ No

Do you want the repast information announced at the end of the service? /___/ Yes /___/ No

REPAST LOCATION:

Address ____

____

City ____State _____Zip Code __________

Contact name____

Phone ____

Date _______________________________ Time _______________________________

NOTE: It is the responsibility of the family to secure a facility for the repast.

Funeral Service Check List

(To Be Used as a Guide)

<u>**NOTE**</u>**: VOLUNTEER STAFFING CAN INCLUDE THE FOLLOWIGN PEOPLE:** Facility Director, Deacons, Safety Team, Sanctuary Attendants (Ushers), Greeters, Ministers, Health Professionals, Operations Staff, Production Staff and Special Needs Ministry)

ITEMS NEEDED

1. **Podium** placed in the lobby area for the Memorial Registry

2. **Memorial Service** — Set Up small table to be placed in front of Pulpit.

3. **Easels** — Pictures can be placed in the lobby or to left of casket.

4. **Videotaping** — Based on availability of staff and capability of reproduction.

5. **Video Presentations** — Limited to 3 to 5 minutes; family must notify staff to valid equipment capability.

6. **Programs** — Requested to be delivered prior to funeral service.

7. **Funeral Memorial Registry or Sign in Book** — Placed on the podium in the lobby by Funeral Director.

8. **Flowers** — All floral deliveries should be placed to the left or right of casket or urn.

THE VOLUNTEERS NEEDED:

1. **Minister of Music** — will be referred all music requests from the family for coordination.

2. **The Deacons** – A deacon is assigned by Head Deacon and stationed at the front of Sanctuary to assist program participants up and down the stairs leading to the podium.

3. **The Facilities Operator** — will check room temperature for room comfort whether heat or air conditioner.

4. **The Deacons** — will arrive one hour or thirty minutes early to meet for prayer and receive and the hearse, limousines or individual family cars.

5. **The Deacons** —will open and close doors of the Facility and check for on-site safety.

6. **Ushers** — will arrive 30 minutes prior to service time for prayer and receive their positions or assigned station.

7. **Greeters** — Will arrive 30 minutes prior to service time for prayer and receive their positions or assigned station.

8. **Ministers** — Will arrive 30 minutes prior to service time for prayer and designated seating assignments.

9. **Health Professionals will arrive 30 minutes prior to service time for prayer and designated seat assignment.**

10. **Operations Staff will arrive 30 minutes prior to service time for prayer and designated seat assignment.**

11. **Production Staff will arrive one hour to 30 minutes prior to service time for prayer and to check the video and CD received from the family members to test equipment capability.**

12. **Special Needs Ministry Staff will arrive 30 minutes early for prayer and to accommodate family members who have disabilities (ADA).**

Memorial Program Example

This should be helpful and should give you an outline from which to use as a guide. Below is a complete **Template Format** for **a Memorial Funeral Program**:

FRONT OF PROGRAM

The Information to include on the front of program includes:

- Full name

- Dates of birth and death

- Time, date and place of funeral

- Name of priest, minister or other dignitary officiating the service.

- Contact information such as a phone number or website address.

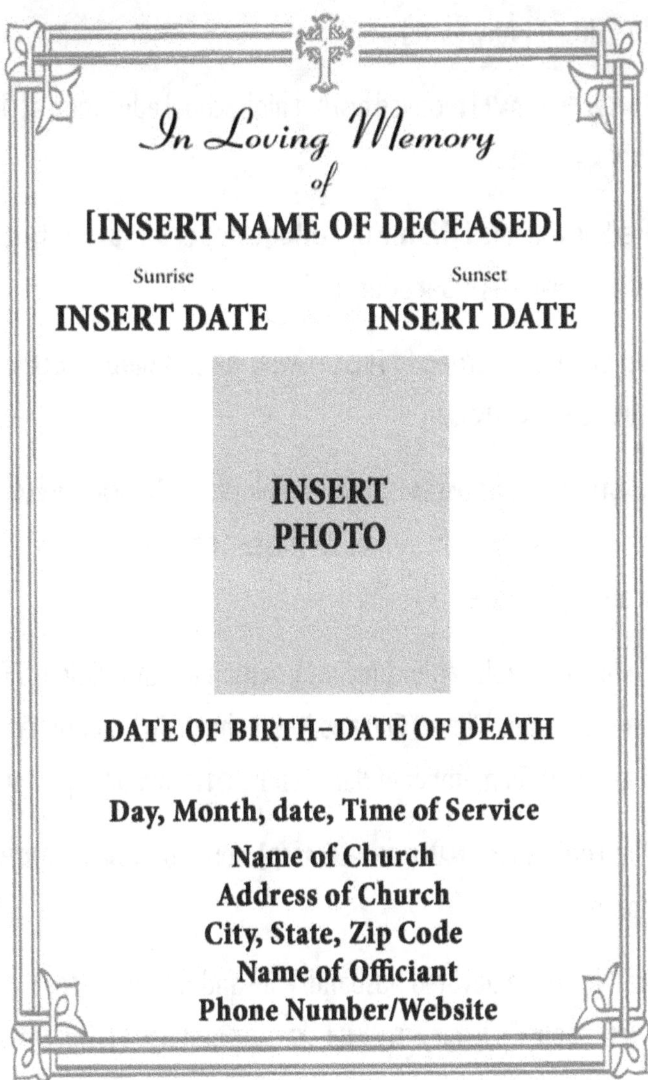

FIRST INSIDE PAGE OF MEMORIAL PROGRAM: OBITUARY

The section of the Memorial Program can include an obituary, life reflections, poetry or other things unique to the deceased. A template for some information you might want to include follows:

SAMPLE OBITUARY (CAN BE USED AS A TEMPLATE)

The Deceased was born on [INSERT DATE] to proud parents, [FATHER'S FULL NAME] and [MOTHER'S FULL NAME]. in [INSERT CITY AND STATE].

[DECEASED NAME] received his/her high school education at [INSERT SCHOOL NAME] From [INSERT DATE RANGE] in [INSERT CITY AND STATE].

He/She attended **[Name of College or Secondary School]** From **[insert Date Range]** in[INSERT CITY AND STATE] and received a **[insert degree]**.

He/She was married to [INSERT WIFE OR HUSBAND'S FULL NAME] for [INSERT NUMBER OF YEARS]. They have [INSERT NUMBER OF CHILDREN].

[INSERT NAME OF DECEASED] was employed by [INSERT EMPLOYER NAME] and worked as a [INSERT JOB TITLE OR DESCRIPTION OF JOB]. He/She retired in [INSERT RETIREMENT YEAR]. (You may also include some information about his/her working life here.)

Final paragraph can include information about religious life, hobbies, memberships, club affiliations, etc. For example: Kenneth loved God and it was shown in his Christian walk with God. He had very strong faith in God. Spouse was a faithful member of Name Church. He loved his pastor and his church members.

The Lord called [NAME OF DECEASED] home on [DAY, MONTH, YEAR]. He/She answered in the quietness of his/her home.

He/She was a devoted Husband/Wife and Father/Mother: He will be remembered by [INSERT CHILDREN'S NAMES, THEIR SPOUSE'S NAME, CITY AND STATE OF RESIDENCE], [INSERT SIBLINGS' NAMES, CITY AND STATE OF RESIDENCE], [NUMBER OF GRANDCHILDREN, NIECES, NEPHEWS COUSINS, ETC.], and [NAME OF CHURCH FAMILY].

SECOND INSIDE PAGE OF MEMORIAL PROGRAM: ORDER OF SERVICE

Items to include in the order of service include, but are not restricted to:

- Processional
- Prayer
- Scripture
- Musical Selection/Solo
- Condolences
- Remarks
- Video
- Silent Reading of Obituary
- Eulogy
- Recessional

SAMPLE PAGE

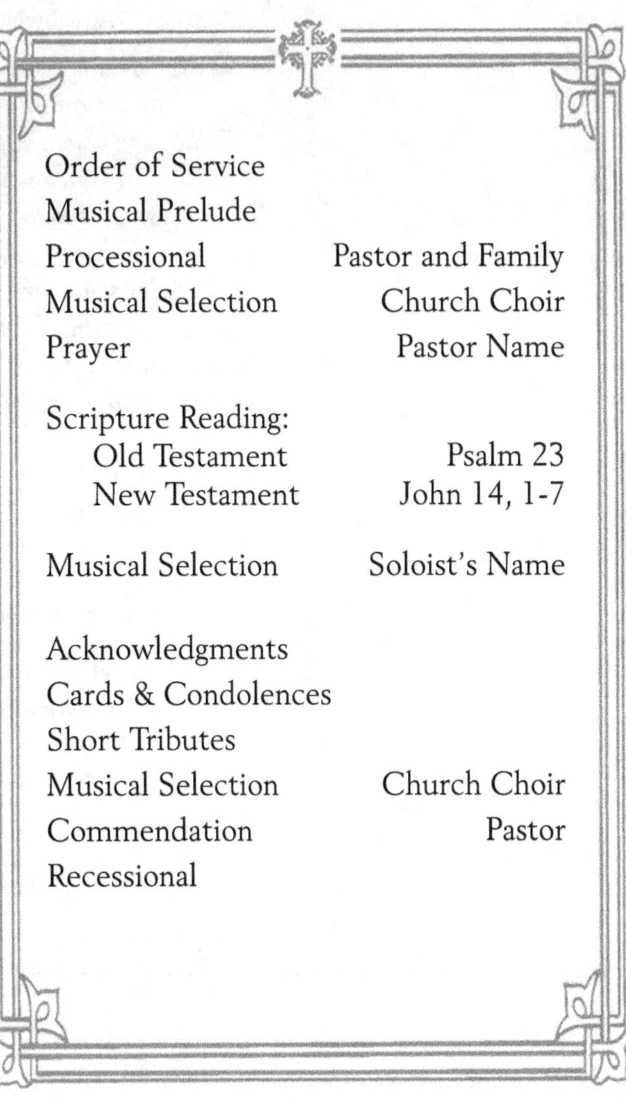

Order of Service
Musical Prelude
Processional   Pastor and Family
Musical Selection   Church Choir
Prayer   Pastor Name

Scripture Reading:
    Old Testament   Psalm 23
    New Testament   John 14, 1-7

Musical Selection   Soloist's Name

Acknowledgments
Cards & Condolences
Short Tributes
Musical Selection   Church Choir
Commendation   Pastor
Recessional

SAMPLE BACK PAGE OF MEMORIAL PROGRAM

Acknowledgment

[SAMPLE] *Perhaps you sang a lovely song,
or sat quietly in a chair.
Perhaps you sent a flower or a plant,
if so we saw it there
Perhaps you spoke the kindest words,
as any friend could say
Perhaps you were not there at all,
just praying for us on this day
Whatever you did to console our family
We thank you so much, whatever the part.*

A special thank you to **[INSERT PASTOR NAME]**, our loving family members and many kind friends.

The Family of **[NAME OF DECEASED]**

Services entrusted to:
[INSERT MORTUARY NAME]
[INSERT MORTUARY ADDRESS]
[INSERT MORTUARY CITY, STATE AND ZIP CODE]

Interment: Private or Public

Repast **[INSERT LOCATION AND TIME]**

Traditional Program Example

This should be helpful and should give you an outline from which to use as a guide. Below is a complete **Template Format** for **a Traditional Funeral Program**:

FRONT OF PROGRAM

The Information to include on the front of program includes:

- Full name

- Dates of birth and death

- Time, date and place of funeral

- Name of priest, minister or other dignitary officiating the service.

- Contact information such as a phone number or website address.

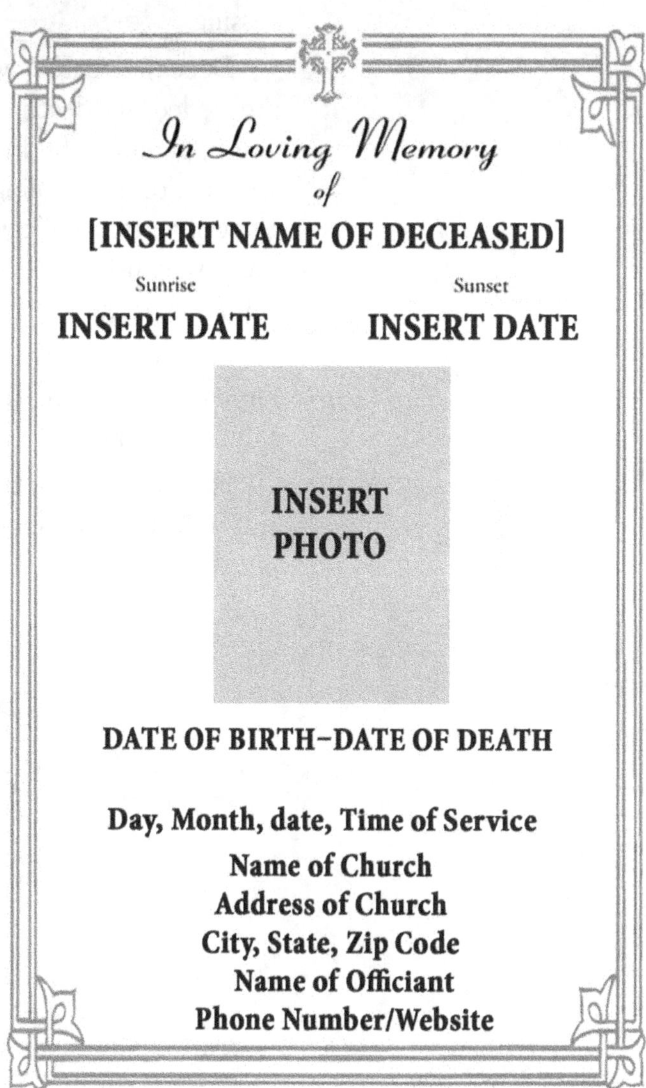

SECOND INSIDE PAGE OF TRADITIONAL PROGRAM: OBITUARY

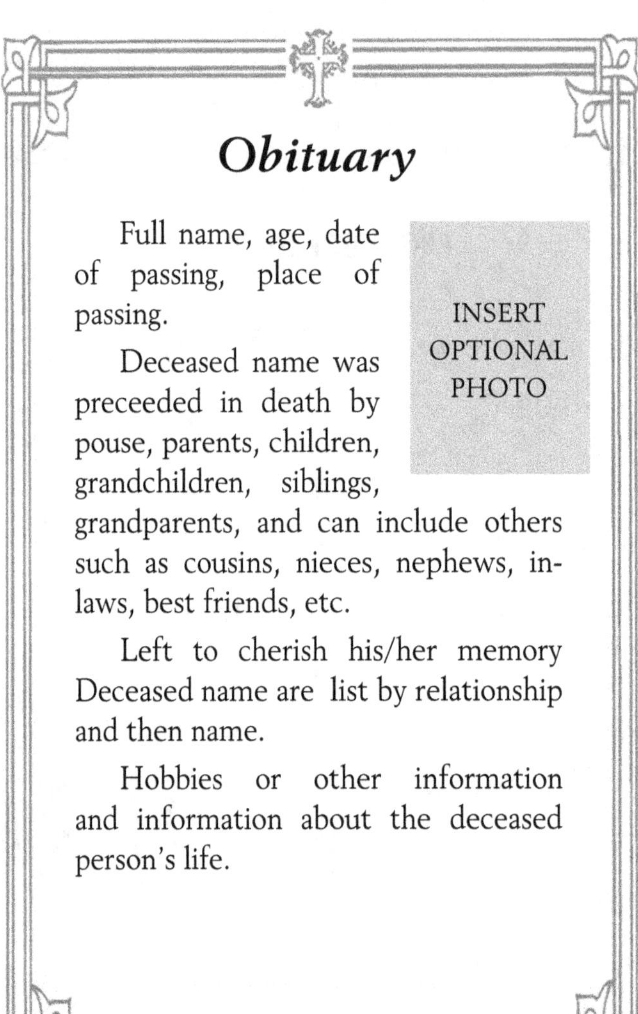

Obituary

Full name, age, date of passing, place of passing.

Deceased name was preceeded in death by pouse, parents, children, grandchildren, siblings, grandparents, and can include others such as cousins, nieces, nephews, in-laws, best friends, etc.

Left to cherish his/her memory Deceased name are list by relationship and then name.

Hobbies or other information and information about the deceased person's life.

THIRD INSIDE PAGE OF TRADITIONAL PROGRAM: ORDER OF SERVICE

Items to include in the order of service include, but are not restricted to:

- Processional
- Prayer
- Scripture
- Musical Selection/Solo
- Condolences
- Remarks
- Video
- Silent Reading of Obituary
- Eulogy
- Final Viewing
- Recessional

SAMPLE PAGE

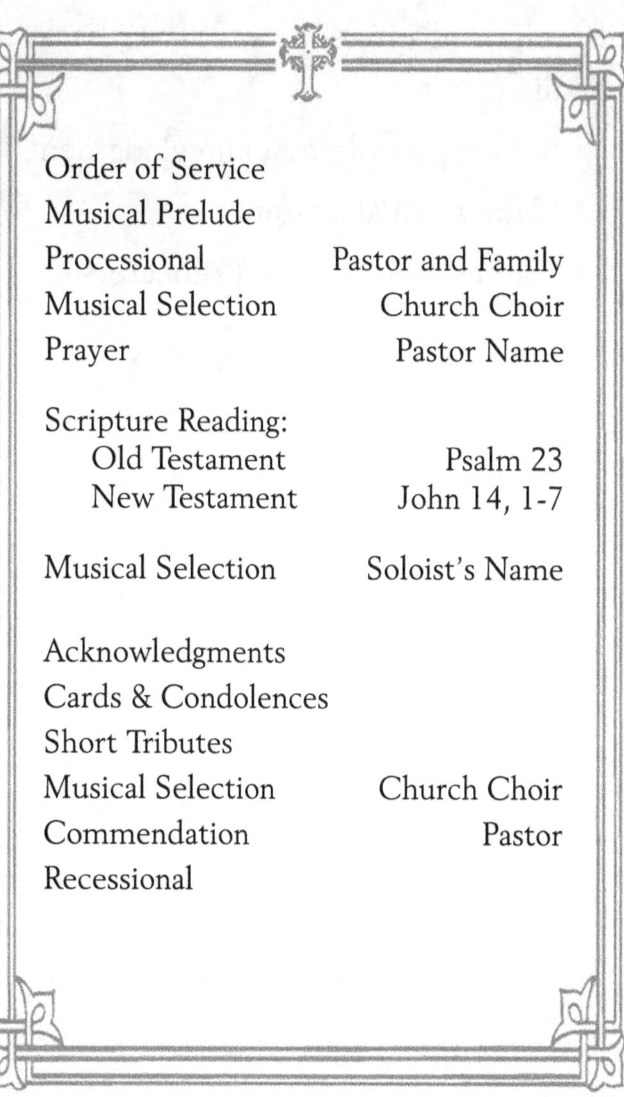

LAST PAGE OF TRADITIONAL PROGRAM (TO BE USED AS A GUIDE)

A traditional program has the same information on the front, but includes different information on the back, including:

- A more complete Acknowledgment
- Names of Pallbearers
- Names of Honorary Pallbearers

Acknowledgment

Insert Acknowledgment text

May God Bless Each Of You!
The Family

Active Pallbearers

Insert Names of Active Pallbearers

Honorary Pallbearers

**Insert Names of
Honorary Pallbearers**

Interment

Insert Interment Location

Will Those Driving In The Procession
Please Turn On Headlights For Safety.

Arrangements

**Insert Name of Funeral Home
Address, and Other
Pertinent Contact Information**

Obituary

(Common elements in a traditional obituary)

An obituary is the synopsis of your life story.

1. Name of deceased person

2. When born, date

3. Place

4. Names of parents (State if preceded in death; as well as any sisters/brothers preceded in death)

5. Education

6. Organizations: Fraternities/Sororities/Eastern Star/Masons, etc.

7. Marriage(s)

8. Children born to the marriage(s)

9. Served in Armed Services

10. Work history

11. Religious Affiliation

12. Hobbies

13. Passed away (date) (place)

14. Leave to cherish memories — spouse, children, etc.

List family members, name, city, and state. Include this for parents, grandparents, husband/wife, sisters, brothers, aunt, uncles, nieces, nephews, cousins, god-daughter; god-son, extended family.

How to Write an Obituary

PARAGRAPH ONE

The first paragraph should contain the name and death announcement:

- Full name of the deceased

- Age at passing

- Date of passing

- Place of passing

Example: John Raymond Doe, age 98, a resident of hometown (list place of residence) left this world on January 27, 2021.

PARAGRAPH TWO

This paragraph lists those who preceded the deceased in death.

This section is commonly ordered as follows: spouse, parents, children, grandchildren, siblings, grandparents, and can include others such as cousins, nieces, nephews, in-laws, best friends, etc.

Example: John was predeceased in death by his beloved wife Twyla, parents John Sr. and Mabel, grandparents Marcus and Beulah...

PARAGRAPH THREE

This paragraph lists surviving family members.

The survivors are listed in the same order as those who preceded the deceased in death.

Common phrasing includes: "Left to cherish his/her memory" are, (Deceased Name) is survived by, or Left to mourn are.

Example: John is survived by his beloved wife Twyla, parents John Sr. and Mabel, Daughter Macy, son Joseph, and grandchildren (they can be named or not), nieces, nephews and friends.

PARAGRAPH FOUR

This paragraph lists all funeral information, including information about visitations, wakes, and viewings, as well as interment. The date, time, location and names of officiants of these events should be listed.

Example: The funeral service will be Wednesday, January 29, 2021 at church or funeral home name, at 1 p.m. Father Bill Bishop will officiate. Interment will follow in the cemetery name.

PARAGRAPH FIVE

This is the closing paragraph in a traditional short form obituary.

The closing paragraph can contain information about charities that people may donate to in lieu of flowers, as well as any acknowledgements from the family.

Example: In lieu of flowers, donations can be made in John's Memory to the Charity Name, Charity Full Mailing Address. The family would like to thank the staff at the Hospital for the wonderful care John received while treated there.

PARAGRAPH SIX

This paragraph is optional and contains information about the deceased's life.

This section can contain information about Friends, School affiliations, Hobbies, achievements, funny stories, etc.

Example: John attended Specific High School and went on to work at Name of Company for 35 years doing heavy construction. He loved fishing and hunting, and everyone will always remember his trophy bass. After he retired, John became a dedicated Hospice volunteer who helped many families.

ADDITONAL OPTIONAL OBITUARY COMPONENT

You may also wish to include a photo of the deceased to go with the obituary.

NOTE: *The contents of this section are intended as a basic guide for composing an obituary. The obituary for your loved one may be written in any way you choose. If you require assistance in writing the obituary, you can contact the funeral home for assistance.*

Dr. Thelma Manning Hall, Ph.D.
Author

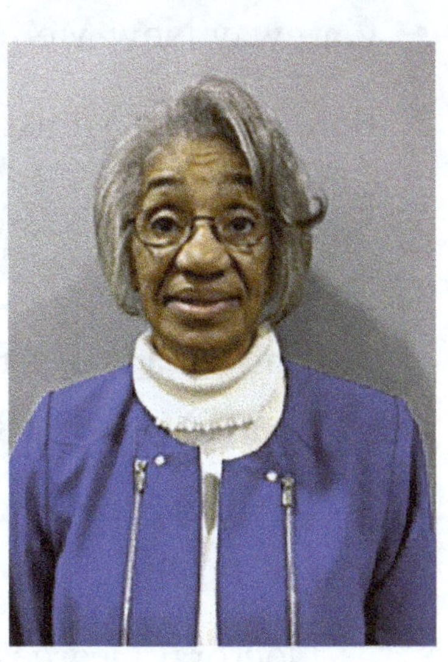

- Married to Charles Hall, Jr.

- Mother: Son, two daughters, three granddaughters, one great granddaughter.

- Christian: Baptized believer, and Filled with the Holy Ghost, 1953. Active in leadership positions at local, state and national levels: Chicago, IL; Kansas City, MO; St. Louis, MO; Huntsville, AL; Las Vegas, NV

- Indiana Avenue Pentecostal Church, Church Secretary; IL (1966–1968)

- Bethesda Temple, Sisterhood, Temperance Group Leader of 65 Ladies; and Usher in charge concurrently 27 years

- District Council Elected two terms as Secretary; Chicago, IL(1964-1968)

- Pentecostal Assemblies of the World, Inc., Elected two terms (Unopposed): set a precedent); Wrote and published the first NYPU Constitution and Bylaws booklet, (1967-1977)

- Northwest District Council, Kansas City, MO, wrote Constitution and Bylaws booklet (1969)

- Bethesda Temple Church, St. Louis, MO, wrote the Sisterhood Constitution and By-law pamphlets (1975)

- Mountaintop Faith Ministries, Las Vegas, Nevada served in leadership positions as Divisional Director for: Christian Education, Deacons Wives Ministry, Bereavement Ministry, Adult Sunday School Ministry; Senior Eagles in Action Ministry; Titus 2 Men & Women Ministry, Counseling Ministry (2001-2011)

- MFM Student Ministries, Tutoring Program, Facilitator (2007-2019)

- Gateway New Members Class, Facilitator (2019)

- Bereavement Ministry Training Coordinator (2019-2021)

- Educator: Graduated with honors at the elementary, secondary and college levels.

  <u>Undergraduate</u>: Bachelor of Science, University of Missouri, St. Louis, St. Louis, MO (1988)

  <u>Graduate</u>: Secondary Education, University of Missouri, St. Louis, St. Louis, MO(1996)

  <u>Doctoral Degrees</u>: Theology, Philosophy, Grief Counseling, Administration, Life Coach Certification, California University of Theology, Englewood, CA (2018)

  <u>Doctoral Degrees</u>: Christian Counseling Administration and Christian Grief Counseling Aenon Bible College, West Coast, of the Pentecostal Assemblies of the World, Inc., Recommended by Board of Directors, Englewood, California. (2018)

- Author of two books: *A Beacon of Light on Grief, Cracking the Code Using This "How To" Handbook Guide* and *Charles Edward Davis, D. D., A Servant's Life: The Chronology.* Both books are available on Amazon and where books are sold.

- Speaker: Preparation for the Future, Nevada District Council, Las Vegas, Nevada Creating a Bereavement Ministry Seminar, Indiana Avenue Pentecostal Church of God, Inc., Chicago, Illinois (2019)

- Community Activist: Introduced Mrs. Michelle Obama, who spoke to all of the volunteers in the entire State of Nevada on a telephone conference call.

- Invited to Attended White House Dinner by President & Mrs. Barack Obama (2012)

- State of Missouri, Board of Embalmers and Funeral Directors, No.4385, Chapter 333, to pursue the practice of the profession of Funeral Directing in accordance with the requirement of the law, License Funeral Director, St. Louis, Missouri (16 Nov 1977 — Inactive Status)

Visit the author's website:

AuthorThelmaHallPhD.com

Email the author: authorthelmamhall@gmail.com

Contact the author by mail:

Thelma Hall, Ph.D.
P. O. Box 336606
North Las Vegas, NV 89033

www.ingramcontent.com/pod-product-compliance
Lightning Source LLC
Chambersburg PA
CBHW080308030726
47593CB00009B/2682